My First Canvas

My First Canvas

Beginner's guide to the world of canvas paintings

Jyoti Arora

Title : My First Canvas

Author & Artist : Jyoti Arora

To the Readers,

May you find happiness!

I wish you a blissful life, good health, more wealth, a peaceful mind, and true dreams.

Artists are just children who refuse to put down their crayons –
Al Hirschfeld

Contents

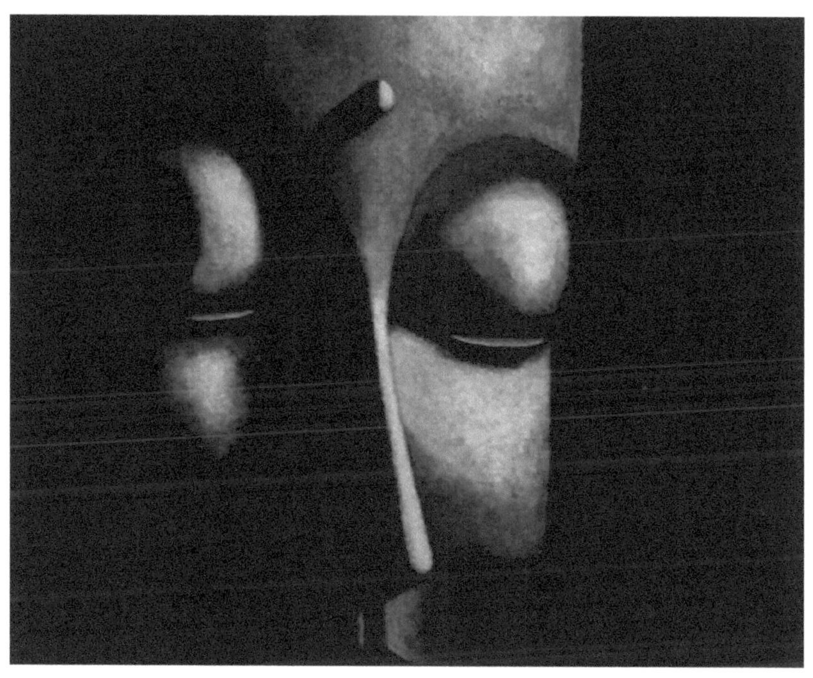

Life is your prayer!
12"x16"
Acrylic on canvas

Preface

Standing alone at the slope of a mountain, covered in snow, she looked for footprints leading to the peak. But the snowfall that has been falling since last night has covered up all the traces.

When she turned to look around, all she could see was pure white everywhere. She was unable to distinguish where the mountain ended and the sky began. As snowflakes brushed the leaves of the forest trees all around her, it appeared as though she was walking on clouds and surrounded by thousands of windchimes ringing rhythmically.

She leaned against a tree and pondered how a fulfilling work, fun social life, travel, and a caring family, had all been a nice bargain. She took out the only chocolate bar she brought with her and ate her meal. The next thought changed her life forever – What if I take just one little step!

I will go through that 1000-mile journey which I began by taking that single step, 10 years ago.

Hello, I'm Jyoti Arora, and I'm an artist.

I've been painting since I was a young child, but I stopped when I graduated and began working in the corporate world.

I always wanted to open an exhibition, but I never had the courage to pick up a paintbrush again until one day, something changed. And I made the decision to pursue my love of art, produce masterpieces, and fulfill my desire to hold an exhibition.

This book is for those who are passionate about art but are unsure of where to begin.

Getting Started

Grandma Moses began painting when she was in her 70s. She did not have time to pursue her love of painting because of her demanding farm life. She didn't pick up the brush again and begin making the iconic pieces until she was 78 years old.

An art collector saw her works in the window of a pharmacy. Three of her paintings were featured in the exhibition "Contemporary Unknown American Painters" at the Museum of Modern Art in New York. Two years later, Otto Kallir's Galerie St. Etienne in New York hosted her first solo exhibition.

That was only the beginning of her career.

She released her autobiography, My Life's History, when she was 92 years old. There she stated "I look back on my life like a good day's work, it was done, and I feel satisfied with it. I was happy and contented; I knew nothing better and made the best out of what life offered. And life is what we make it, always has been, always will be "

Monet began painting in his forties. The first cookbook by Julia Child was released when she was in her forties. Boman Irani didn't begin his film career till he was 41 years old.

What do they all have in common? They never lost sight of their dream.

The mental block is entirely in your head!

Most people procrastinate for a variety of reasons:

"Everyone advises, "Follow your passion!" Do you realize how difficult it might be to pursue one's passion? It requires time, commitment, investment, and many other things, and I'm not even sure if I'll succeed."
"My work does not allow me to devote enough time to such endeavors."
"I never pursued my passion, and it has now faded over time."

It can be difficult to take the initial step. It can be quite challenging to carve out time for ourselves given the daily tasks we must complete in order to earn a living. There are countless reasons why you shouldn't pursue your passion, but there is only one way to take that first step: by getting started.

How?

I was eager to begin again after returning from that mountain top. I went to the market without giving it much thought and bought a small set of oil paints and a set of five round brushes. I initially assumed that would be sufficient. However, without research, it was a fruitless endeavor. I didn't know how to begin using oil paint; should I mix it with water or just pour it as-is?

But as time went on, I learned that oil paints require a thinner, such as linseed oil, while painting.

It's crucial to decide on your supplies before beginning your first painting. Which style of painting do you want to create? Will it require more than one day to finish? If so, does it call for a lot of mixing or do you prefer an abstract with multiple layers?

You can find the answers to these questions and create your first canvas painting by following the next 5 steps.

____

Step 1 : Well-lit space

Choose a location for your painting session.

- This location could be your art or yoga studio, a nearby park, or one of your home's bedrooms, kitchen tables, living rooms, balconies, etc.
- Remove all clutter from the area and the immediate vicinity. Maintain order and cleanliness.
- It needs to be well-lit because one of the key elements in art is light.
- Along with the painting, the area should allow you to store your tools and completed projects.

Step 2 : Medium - Acrylic, Oil or Watercolor

Choose your medium from watercolor, oil, or acrylic.
For the paintings in this book, I used acrylic paints. Acrylic is simple to begin with, and if something goes awry, you can always paint another layer on top of it.

Key difference between Acrylic and Oil

	Acrylic	**Oil**
Base	Water-based Waterproof when dry	Oil-based
Drying Time	Fast drying time – few minutes to few hours	Slow drying time – hours to days or weeks
Blending	Difficult to blend once the paint is dried	Easy to blend even the next day as drying time is longer
Layers	Easy to apply another layer within few minutes	Wait for next day to apply another layer
Space	Works well in both small and open spaces	Needs open space with ventilation as fumes from thinner are strong and irritate your skin in confined space.
Lightfast	Acrylic do not fade in time	Oil turns yellow over time due to process of oxidation
Cleaning tools	Easy to clean with water	Need other media to clean oil paint.
Cost	Affordable	Expensive than acrylic

Step 3 : Supplies

Colors

- Purchase your initial set of colors once you've chosen the medium. Pick a minimal set of colors instead of using too many at once. Depending on your painting needs and budget, choose a modest pack of 6 or 12 colors rather than larger tubes.
- Every person has a different aesthetic and set of criteria for selecting colors. But until you complete a few paintings, you won't be able to tell which hue will become your favorite.
- In all of your paintings, you'll always utilize a select few colors. When you have decided whatever colors you prefer, you can later purchase a larger tube of those hues.

Canvas

- o   There are numerous varieties of canvases, including universal canvas, absorbent canvas, and oil canvas. Cotton canvas is the most popular type of canvas and is available in the following varieties:
    a. Stretched canvas – A stretched canvas is one that has been attached to a wooden frame.
    b. Canvas board – Canvas material is adhered to a wooden board to create a canvas board.
    c. Canvas roll – A canvas roll is just a roll of canvas fabric.

- o   After making your decision, unless you intend to prime your canvas yourself, choose a pre-primed canvas.

Why should my canvas be primed? – Primer offers canvas a smooth surface to paint on and increases the painting's lifespan. Without it, color might sink into the canvas and leave blotches on the surface.

Brushes

o Brushes can be divided into two categories: round brush and flat brush.
There are several options available; however, do not let this fact overwhelm you. Choose the basic selection of brushes while keeping in mind the medium you've chosen.

o Natural or Synthetic brush
Synthetic brushes, which are made of synthetic fiber, are better suited for water-based paints like acrylic. For oil paintings, natural is better.

	Synthetic	**Natural**
Material	Made from synthetic fibers like nylon, polyester	Made from animal hair
Suitable for	Best for water-based paints	Best for applying oil paint
Cost	Affordable	Expensive than synthetic brush
Cleaning	Easy to clean	Difficult to clean

o Start with the basic 6 brush types:

a. Round brush (medium): A medium-sized round brush is best for powerful strokes and fine detailing.
b. Detail or liner brush (small): To add fine lines or facial expressions to portraits as well as other details to your artwork. I also sign my paintings with this brush.

c. Flat brush (medium, 1~ inch): It is used to paint with lengthy, precise strokes.
d. Filbert brush: Flat brush with rounded edges. Good for blending in paintings.
e. Bright brush: It's a flat brush with short bristles. I've used it in a lot of my abstract artwork. The color is laid out in a square shape with clean edges.
f. Fan Brush: It is mostly used to paint leaves on trees or create texture to grass, earth, beaches, and rocks.

o Washing your brushes after painting: Always remember to do this after your day of work. For acrylic paints, I advise washing the brush same day after usage because the dried paint can harm the bristles.

Palette Knives

- o   Palette knife is a steel blunt blade which is used for mixing paint, applying paint on canvas, adding texture to your artwork, etc.
- o   Two types of palette knife
    - a.   A flat knife that is good for blending colors has rounded edges similar to a putty knife.
    - b.   A pointed-tipped knife ideal for use when painting on canvas.
- o   I've never used a flat knife myself. Small amounts of paint can be mixed with ease with a pointed-tip knife. Knives have predominantly been used in my abstract works.
- o   A few quick pointers for choosing knives:
    - a.   Flexible but strong blade
    - b.   Comfortable handle
    - c.   Long and straight edge

You've got your supplies. What is the first thing you wish to paint?

Think about the first painting you want to produce for a moment. It will help you think more creatively if you choose a quiet and peaceful place or do something to ease your mind. You can start a small or you can run wild with your imagination.

If you want to paint, just paint!

Inspiration will find you!

It began with a strange feeling, similar to the feeling you get when you leap off a cliff while swimming or even while river rafting, just multiply it to 100 folds!

Determined to go into that giant unknown with trembling hands, I got ready to take that leap of faith. The air smelled fresh and cool under the warmth of the winter sun. I closed my eyes, took a deep breath, and jumped into the magnificent ocean.

When your senses like smell or hearing are blocked, your eyes will grab all your attention to see the most beautiful sight. The only sound that you can hear comes from within—your breath! With each and every breath you take, you go further into ecstasy, and then you'll realize the 6th sense: that feeling from within, the most powerful of all, that soulful feeling that cannot be described in words.

It was the most beautiful and peaceful place on earth. Everything moved in slow motion; it was all so blue, so green, yet so colorful.

No matter how high and noisy the waves may seem at the surface, 40 feet under the ocean, there's just the sound of your breath, calm, and a peaceful mind!

Scuba was the beginning of the most fascinating experience. A whole new journey begins when you get submerged in the water. It's a different world altogether, one that comes with a million possibilities to explore.

All I could see were colors in that silent ocean, a blank canvas ready to be painted.

Step 4: My first canvas

Rainy day – Selective color painting

The materials used in each painting are entirely up to you; you can select any color and select from a variety of options. For instance: Canvas board or canvas cloth can be used in place of stretched canvas. You may choose to use a paintbrush in place of a palette knife.

First time with a palette knife? Don't be intimidated by the knife; once you know how to handle it, it's extremely easy.

Material used in this artwork:
    a. 10" by 12" canvas board
    b. Acrylic Paints: Black, titanium white, and scarlet lake red
    c. Flat brush (medium), palette knife (small)

Most of the painting will be done in black and white. The brush strokes will be straight up and down to give that rainy effect. It'll be lighter in the center and darker on the sides.

Steps:

Background color –
- On a palette, we place a small amount of black and white paint.
- Next, take a flat brush that is about one inch in size. Simply moisten the brush's tip.

- o Fill the brush with white paint and a tiny bit of black pigment.
- o Place the color in the middle and begin painting. If you accidentally used too much black, simply add additional white and apply it with the same strokes. Leave it alone if you notice any black streaks on white or white streaks on black.
- o We'll now move to the edges and work on both sides simultaneously. Take some white again but add a few more specks of that black color this time. Starting where you left off, paint one side. Repeat your previous up-and-down brushstrokes.
- o Next, let's do the same thing on the other side.
- o Put some more paint on your brush, but this time use more black and less white.
- o Repeat the same strokes on the opposite side.
- o For the final section, fill the brush with black and a touch of white. Use the same strokes to cover the canvas.

City and Horizon –
- o Next, place the horizon by drawing a line with the palette knife. The palette knife will only make a small imprint on the color because it is still wet, giving us a faint indication of the horizon.
- o If you do not want to use the knife, then simply use your flat brush.
- o To give the illusion of a street, we will construct buildings on either side and leave the center empty.
- o We'll use a color that is similar to what we used on the edges; it need not be exactly the same shade; it could be a little lighter or darker.
- o Mix a little bit of white and a little bit of black paint on the knife or brush's edge. Just to the left of the center, place it on the canvas. Make sure the paint contacts the

canvas without exerting too much pressure. Then, with one stroke, lower the knife/brush. It doesn't need to be flawless, so don't stress about the edges. It will disappear below the horizon, giving the impression that the buildings are reflected in the wet street.
  o Add a couple more streaks to the painting; they can be overlapping and of various sizes. This will create the appearance of nearby buildings.
  o Continue with darker streaks on the sides, almost solid back on the extreme ends, and keep the color light in either side in the center.

Water reflection –
  o Dab the tiniest speck of white paint on the edge of a knife in the center, beginning at the horizon. Dab until no more paint appears.
  o If you're applying paint using a brush, get the thinnest flat brush you can find and only use the flat edge of the brush to apply the paint. Starting at the center of the horizon, dab it as flatly as possible until no more paint comes out.
  o Once more, take a small amount of paint, combine white and black to create a light grey color, and begin dabbing from the horizon to the bottom.
  o To draw the lines on the extremes to the right and left, use just black.

Highlight the subject –
  o Go for any color of your choice, except for black and white.
  o You can create any subject, including a flower in the street, car, traffic light, horse cart, any shop, etc.
  o A woman in a red dress is my subject in this painting.
  o Place a tiny amount of red paint on the pointed blade of the palette knife. Set the color where the lady's shoulder

will be and spread it in an inverted V shape with one stroke, just like frosting on a cake. The fold in her clothing will resemble the lines made by the palette knife.

- o   If you're unsure about using a palette knife, make the outfit with the tiniest round detail brush.
- o   Apply some black paint to a detail brush and use it to create her hair and legs.

Rainy Day – Woman in Red!
10"x12"
Acrylic & Oil on canvas

First Rain!
16"x12"
Acrylic on canvas

Different types of backgrounds

Creating different background styles for paintings

- o Paintbrush: The options for designing a background are virtually limitless. Using basic brush strokes, like we did when painting in the rain, is one technique. You may try using horizontal, crisscross strokes instead of the vertical ones we used earlier. The subject in front can also be highlighted by painting the background a solid color or blending the paint with a smooth brush like a filbert.

- o Textured Background: You can use any material to create a background for your painting, including polybags, bubble wrap, scales, sponges, rollers, and scales with jagged edges.

- o Using these supplies is easy; all you need to do is pour some color onto a palette, grab the material, and apply the color. Then begin dabbing it in any shape or pattern onto the canvas.

- o Cling film or polybag - An inventive way utilizing polythene material
  Painting: Abstract – Earth!
  Paint some color on canvas, then use spray bottle to spray a bit of Paint a canvas with some color, add some water with a spray bottle, and top it with a crumpled polybag. Leave it alone till it dries out. Keep in mind that polythene lengthens the drying process, so give it a little more time. Then, remove the material from the canvas to get the desired effect.

- o Sponge – using multiple colors
  Put a few colors on the palette next to one another. In order to get a little of each hue, grab the sponge and dab it in the middle before dabbing it on the canvas. Repeat the procedure and keep dabbing until the canvas, or the required area, is completely filled.

Bliss!
18"x14"
Acrylic on canvas

Bliss!
18"x14"
Acrylic on canvas

Shadows!
24"x16"
Acrylic on canvas

Dreams!
16"x12"
Acrylic on canvas

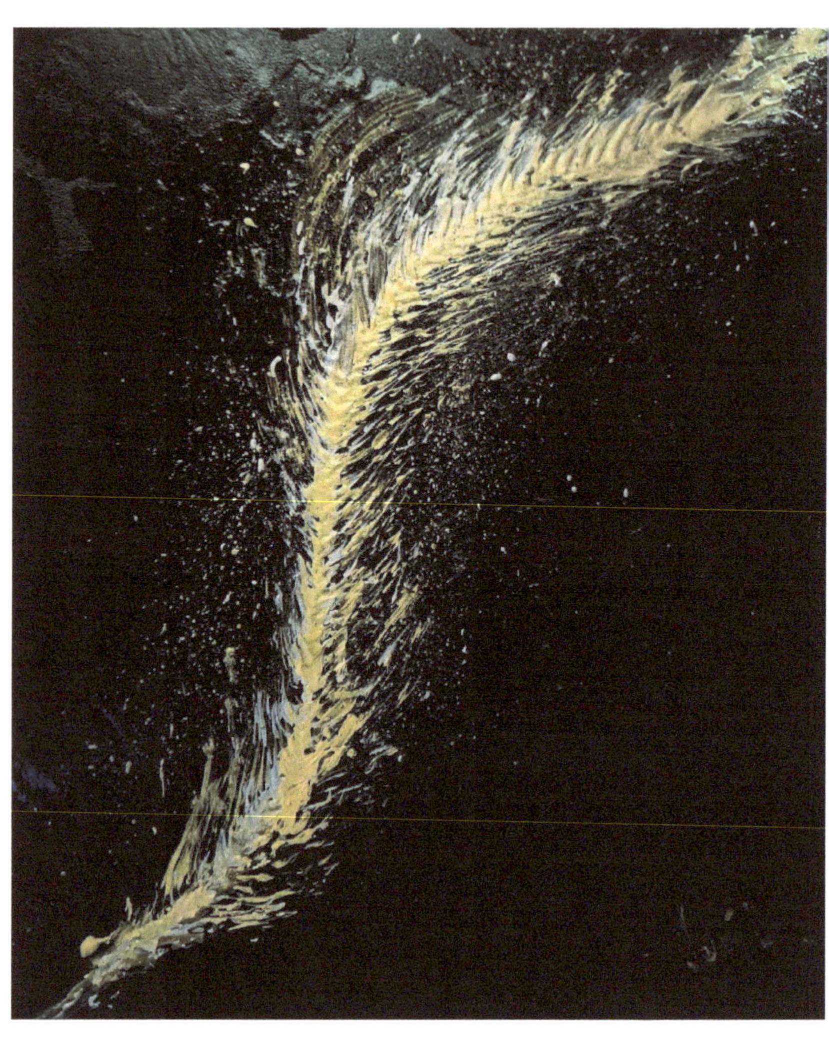

Feather of my wings!
9"x8"
Acrylic on wood

Abstract – Earth!
10"x12"
Acrylic on canvas (Polythene imprint)

Spring – Use of fan brush

Tree painting with a fan brush is a simple and well-known technique. You need one round or flat brush to make the tree trunk; one small round brush for the stems; and one fan brush for the tree leaves.

Steps –
- You can use a circular brush to make the trunk of a tree, or you can use a knife. The edges don't have to be flawless.
- To create a reflection of light effect, draw a white line around the trunk's edges.
- Take some color of your choice on the crescent of the fan brush and start dabbing the crescent where tree leaves are going to be.
- Add more to the middle to make it dense, a little less to the edges, and leave a few crescent-shaped leaves on the ends.
- To make it appear as though some leaves have fallen from the tree, apply the same color to the tree's base.

Spring!
12"x16"
Acrylic on canvas

Midnight Dream!
12"x16"
Acrylic on canvas

Abstract – Bright brush

We'll use a bright brush and a variety of colors to create the background. For the entire backdrop, we'll combine the colors with a simple stroke.

Steps –

- o Choose the colors you want to use for the artwork. Put blobs of those colors wherever you wish on the canvas. If you want the painting to be predominantly red with a greenish blue tint on the opposite side and a light hue in the center. Then split the canvas into three sections and arrange light-colored blobs, such as white or golden ones, in the center, followed by red blobs on one side and blue or green blobs on the other.
- o The first step is best suitable for small to medium size canvas. For large canvas, cover half of the canvas with color blobs and go to step 2. This is because acrylics dry quickly; if you take too long applying the brush as directed, the color blobs may dry out.
- o Use the flat brush to apply the lightest color first. Don't complete the streak in either direction; just place the brush flat on the dot. Leave the square shape exactly as it is. There's no need for the shape to be perfectly square.
- o Remove the brush and reposition it next to the newly formed square. Continue applying these strokes to one side until the entire side of the canvas is covered in square-shaped strokes. When you get to the other color blobs, don't worry about blending; the brush will take care of it.
- o Now, clean the brush's color. Return to the center and move to the opposite side.

- o By this point, your entire canvas should be covered in square-shaped strokes with colors in perfect harmony.
- o Let it dry for an hour.
- o You can create any image you want as your subject or leave it as is.

Dance!
12"x16"
Acrylic on canvas

Just living is not enough!
12"x16"
Acrylic on canvas

Abstract – Painter's tape or Masking Tape

Tape for canvas painting: Painter's tape and masking tape both have a crepe paper backing, touch and feel are the same for both and are suitable for use in canvas painting.
I have used masking tape in my paintings, which gives the same effect as painter's tape.

	Painter's Tape	Masking Tape
Effect on Painting	Does not crinkle and ruin the edges of the line. It does the job with neat and clean effect	It does the same job with clean effect but sometimes the paint could come off if not removed carefully.
Adhesive	Not very strong adhesive, so when removed it does not leave any residue.	Use a bit stronger adhesive than painter's tape, could leave a residue which can be difficult to clean.
Cost	On expensive side	Affordable

Steps –

- o You can either create a background of your choice and use the tape to give it some detail or you can start with the tape directly and create your painting with clean edges.
- o Decide on the pattern and type of paint –

- Pattern – Includes V-shapes, zigzag, straight bars, horizontal bars, multiple squares and Triangles
- Type – Includes Spray painting, palette knife painting, simple brush strokes and many sorts of different boxes.

- After choosing your pattern, grab the tape and stick it to the canvas. To make sure it is firmly adhered, press it down. It will keep the color from bleeding.
- Giving shadow effect: To create a shadow, choose a side from which the light will come; for simplicity, let's say it will come from the right.
- Combine some black and a tiny bit of blue. Take a small brush and some paint, then paint it on the tape's left side. Paint a single line, then use a clean, dry brush to mix the line until it is blurry.
- If you have made many divisions, apply the same method to drawing a blur line to all of the left sides.
- Tape removal: Don't leave the tape on for too long; doing so will cause the paint to chip off. It could result in paint dripping if you remove it too soon while the paint is still wet.
- Once the paint has sufficiently dried, remove the tape. To prevent affecting the color, remove the tape as gently as you can.

Secret Garden!
38"x20"
Acrylic on canvas

State of Mind!
14"x18"
Acrylic on canvas

Abstract – knife painting

Once you begin using a knife to paint, there is no turning back. You'll become addicted on it. That's how gratifying it is.

Once you master the technique, painting with a knife will be a piece of cake.

To begin with, try out a modest set of palette knives. A set of five knives is easily available online. When you experiment with a few knives, you'll discover your favorite one.

- o Start with a small canvas; anywhere between 10" and 16" canvases are ideal. Consider using stretched canvas or canvas board. Paint is easier to apply with a knife on a firm base.
- o Thick paints like acrylic or oil are appropriate for knife painting. To make oil paint thicker, some artists combine oil and cold wax.
- o You can use a knife to blend the colors after placing them on a palette. Then, load the knife with color and apply it to the canvas like you would while frosting a cake.
- o You can also apply color straight to the canvas and spread it with a knife.
- o The procedure is the same whether you use a palette or add the color directly to the canvas.
- o Sweep the paint across the canvas using the long side of the blade while tilting it slightly, just like you would with frosting on a cake or a thick layer of butter on bread.
- o Avoid applying excessive pressure to the knife or you'll scrape off all the pigment. When sweeping the pigment,

always be gentle. Depending on how thin or thick of a
layer you desire, tilt the blade at a 30-to-45-degree
angle.
- o Diverse forms, angles, and pressure levels will result in
  different textures and layers. For instance, when
  painting the red dress in the rainy-day picture, I used the
  knife's pointed side.
- o You may also use knife to produce a similar background
  to what we accomplished with the bright brush.

Techniques –

Impasto technique – Applying heavy layers of paint to a canvas
to create texture
- o Apply color to the canvas in blobs and spread it out into
  a thick layer.
- o You can apply strokes in the same direction or in
  different ways to create a mystic effect.
- o You can always add another layer and a different color
  on top of your existing work to add more texture,
  design, and effect.

Sgraffito technique – Layers and lines
- o Paint the canvas with a layer of color. A second color
  layer should be added on top of the first once it has
  partially dried.
- o Scrape away the top layer to reveal the one underneath.
- o Lines – To scratch the top layer and form lines, angle a
  knife 90 degrees so the sharp edge touches the canvas.

Multiple colors –

____

- o Place the colors on the canvas; the blobs should be close to one another.
- o Use the knife to cut through each hue in one stroke.

Multiple techniques in one painting –

- o You can experiment with several approaches while working on the same artwork. Using knife and brush strokes, for example. Or perhaps use several materials to provide texture.
- o To complete a painting, you don't have to use just one tool. Brush strokes can be used to smudge the edges of the knife paint. Alternately, use a brush or other tool to paint the backdrop, then use a knife to add texture on top of it.

A Colorful Life!
24"x36"
Acrylic on canvas

Behind her eyes!
16"x12"
Acrylic on canvas

Freedom!
12"x12"
Acrylic on canvas

Geometry!
10"x12"
Acrylic on canvas

Seaside!
10"x12"
Acrylic on canvas

Red!
20"x16"
Acrylic on canvas

Multiple canvas painting

Multiple canvas paintings raise the level of interest as compared to a single canvas painting on any mundane subject. Additionally, it is easier to transport than a single large canvas painting.

Steps –
- o Place the canvases adjacent to one another; you can leave them that way or tape them together loosely.
- o If you don't join them with tape, make sure they stay in place while you lay the foundation for painting.
- o Base: Sketch down a quick outline of what you intend to paint on each canvas, moving from one to the next. You can either use a pencil drawing or a paintbrush to outline your artwork.
- o Paint: It could be uncomfortable to paint the canvases together. Your back can hurt if you lay it out on a big surface and decide to paint while bending over. Instead, individually paint each canvas on an easel. Because you've drawn the contour, painting the canvases individually will be easier.
- o After painting the canvases, lay them out one more time to make sure the colors are smoothly flowing from one canvas to the next.

Beatles Abbey!
18"x56" (18"x14" each)
Acrylic on canvas

3 Canvas Painting – Place the canvases adjacent to one another and sketch down the outline

Bliss!
36"x16" (12"x16" each)
Acrylic on canvas

Textured Art

Gesso

It is used to prepare any type of surface for painting, such as canvas, wood panels, and sculptures. It is also frequently used by artists to give their paintings texture.

If you purchase canvas that has not been primed, you can use gesso as a primer to get your canvas ready for painting.

It is made from two or more of the following materials:

I.	Glue/binder
II.	Chalk
III.	Gypsum
IV.	Colorant (usually white paint)

Additionally, gesso can be made at home using chalk or talc, glue, and white paint. The consistency varies depending on whether it is used as a primer or for texture.

Gesso as Primer –

- o Choose gesso that has a fluid-like consistency.
- o Dip the flat wide brush in gesso
- o Apply it uniformly over the entire canvas, including the corners and edges.
- o Give it a few hours to dry.
- o Your canvas is now ready to be painted.

Texture with Gesso –

- o Use gesso with a heavy consistency to add texture.

- It may be used to create anything from light-textured paintings to dense effects like waves, fur, grass, and flowers, as well as entire shapes like human figures and objects.
- Base – Gesso can be used to make a textured base.
  - Scribble or pattern – Apply gesso evenly on canvas, let it dry partially. Then, using a pencil or palette knife, begin scribbling or creating any design you wish.
    Allow it to dry completely before painting over it the next day.
  - Layers – Apply a layer of gesso, let it dry. Add a second layer on top of it to add texture.
- Colored Gesso – You can also experiment with blending colors into the ready gesso to make colored gesso, which can be used as a primer or to create a variety of colored textures. You can experiment with any other color for homemade gesso in place of white pigment.
- Use thick-consistency gesso for heavy shapes like objects, waves, or grass effects. Alternately, adjust the chalk/talc quantity to achieve the desired result.
- Palette knife is the best tool for creating thick effects. You may cut through the edges to create thick effects with granular details.

Multi-technique painting

- o You may create textured abstract art on canvas using a variety of techniques, including gesso, knife painting, and material imprinting.

- o Painting: "Together"
  Stretched canvas – 24"x36"
  Techniques – Gesso, Palette knife, brush.
  For Texture – Hands, sponge, thread, round caps, bubble wrap and paper
    - Apply a thick layer of gesso over the canvas, make sure to cover the sides and corners.
    - To add texture, imprint any pattern or substance onto the gesso while it's still wet. In the "Together" artwork, I used the bare hands of my family members.
    - Once dry, begin painting over it.
    - Use a different color to emphasize the focal point. In this painting, I chose golden yellow to emphasize the hands in the middle.
    - Use dry brush to highlight the effects – Use a knife or brush to apply a little amount of color to the palette. Take a completely dry brush now, and lightly dab it on the palette. Spread the paint on the raised texture of the focal area on the canvas using a very light touch.

Together!
24"x36"
Acrylic on canvas

- o Painting: The last symphony
  Stretched canvas – 36"x24" (26"x12" each canvas)
  Techniques – Palette knife, brush, Gesso
  For texture – Pencil, syringe
  - Apply gesso evenly throughout the canvas, add texture with a pencil, and allow it to dry.
  - Paint the backdrop.
  - Apply paint in blobs to the canvas and use a knife to sweep the paint in the desired pattern.
  - Pour some color into a little container or a bottle cap, then add some water to thin out the acrylic paint and make it watery.
  - To add texture to canvas, fill a syringe with color and dispense it across the surface.

The Last Symphony!
36"x24" (36"x12" each)
Acrylic on canvas

- ○ Painting: Medieval
  Stretched canvas – 10"x12"
  Techniques – Palette knife, brush, Gesso
  For texture – Pencil, sponge

Medieval!
10"x12"
Acrylic on canvas

Plaster of Paris

It's a gypsum-based fine white powder. It is utilized for bandages, casting, and sculpture. Additionally, artists use it to produce textured artwork on canvases, walls, or wooden supports.

Fresco, a plaster method, was used by ancient civilization to create works of art, including the sculptures found in the tombs of Egypt and Morocco, the Greek colonies, the Indian caves and monuments, Sri Lanka, and Rome.

Base material – Canvas or wood?

Wooden panel or plywood – You can build any large body sculpture on a base made of wood; however, adhesion may be problematic when using POP directly on the wood.

Canvas roll – It might not be a good idea to use canvas roll as is. POP can easily break with movement on canvas since it becomes thick when it dries.

Stretched canvas – Canvas that has been stretched across a wooden panel on the sides can be used for light textures but not for full-bodied sculptures on canvas.

Canvas board – A wooden board with canvas cloth put on it. Both heavy body sculptures and light weight textures work well with it.

Mixing Plaster of Paris: When handling POP, put on plastic gloves, preferably disposable ones.

Material –

    I.   A mixing container, cup, or palette, depending on the quantity.
    II.   Plastic/ disposable spoon or spatula
    III.   Plastic sheet or wastepaper/newspaper to cover the area where the plaster will be mixed.
    IV.   Plaster of Paris powder and water.

Steps –

- Take the powder and water in 1:2 ratio. If you want to mix 1 cup of powder, take half a cup of water.
- After adding the water to the container, begin to sprinkle the powder in it one spoon at a time. Use a disposable spoon or spatula to stir it slowly until there are no lumps.
- It'll have a consistency of thick paste, if it's too thick, add more water.
- You will have 10 minutes to apply the mixture in the chosen pattern after it is ready. It will begin to solidify as time passes by.
- Colored mixture – After the third step, you can add any acrylic paint or poster paint to create a colored mixture.

Disposing the left-over POP –

- Don't wash the spoon, spatula, or container you used to mix the POP mixture in the sink, and don't dump the leftover mixture down the drain either. The POP will clog the drain.
- Allow the leftovers to dry before throwing them away with the other materials used in the mixture.

POP – Textured art

- o Scoop some of your prepared mixture onto the canvas. Add another scoop if you need more.
- o Using a spatula or palette knife, spread the paste throughout the canvas. Try to cover as much ground as you can. A spatula can be used for big areas, and a palette knife can be used for small edges.
- o Use a knife's sharp edge or another object with sharp edges to provide texture.
- o Allow it to dry completely.
- o Apply a base color to the canvas's whole surface, including the sides and edges. If you prefer your artwork in white plaster as is, you can paint it white or combine paint and varnish to finish it.
- o If you are using colored POP, then skip directly to the last step – finishing with Varnish.
- o Highlight – Use the same dry brush technique to highlight the raised texture:
  Use a knife or brush to apply a little amount of color to the palette. Take a completely dry brush now, and lightly dab it on the palette. Spread the paint on the raised texture of the focal area on the canvas using a very light touch.

Plaster of Paris bandage – Textured art

If you don't want to deal with the mixture or making the paste, there's good news: you may use POP bandage instead. The use of POP bandages is limited to textured art. The bandage may not be used to make sculptures or molds.

Steps –

- o To make the POP bandage more adherent, you may apply a layer of gesso.
- o Put on your gloves, do not work with POP with your bare hands.
- o Cut the POP bandage roll into the required number of pieces.
    - Use the same pattern when cutting the pieces if you want the painting to have little squares or other shapes of a few inches.
    - You may make it as little or as long as you like, up to 2 feet in length. Anything longer could be challenging to manage. Once you begin using the bandage, you will be able to decide the size that is most comfortable for you.
- o Set a water-filled container to one side.
- o Next, take a single bandage at a time, dunk it in water, let the extra water drip out a little, and then arrange the bandage on the canvas in the desired pattern.
- o Follow the same procedures for each bandage.
- o Wait a day or two before covering it with paint. Coat it with white acrylic if you don't want to color it.

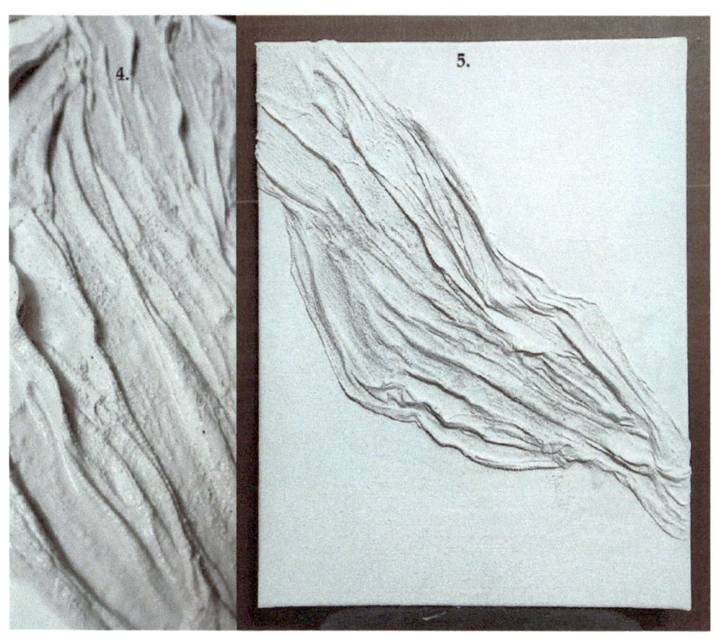

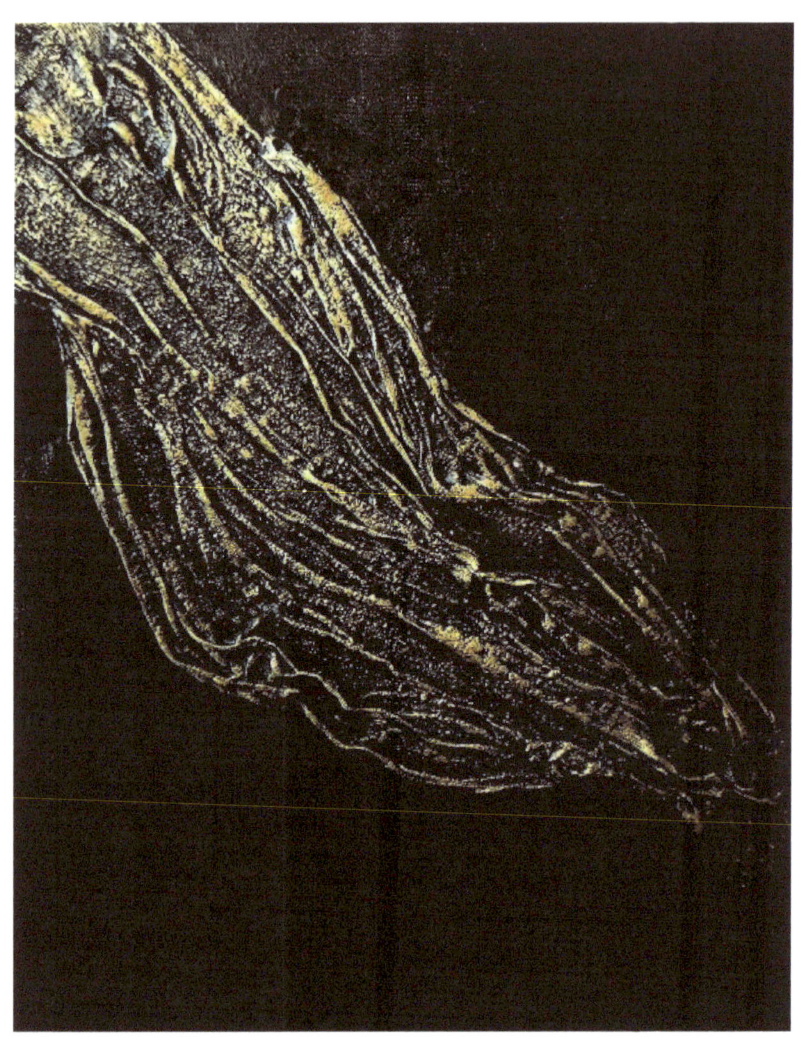

POP Abstract!
20"x16"
Plaster of Paris & Acrylic on canvas

Plaster of Paris molds

- o Apply a coat of petroleum jelly inside the mold.
- o Fill the mold with the POP mixture and allow it to dry.
  POP may require up to 24 to 48 hours to fully set,
  depending on the size and nature of the mold.
- o After it has dried, remove the solid POP

Step 5: The final touch

Finish

How will you know when your artwork is complete?

You'll always feel that some tiny details need to be touched up, perhaps with a few extra strokes or a splash of color. Sometimes you complete the painting you intended to achieve but are still not pleased.
Until you feel satisfied with your artwork, the painting will remain incomplete.

I could spend hours just looking at an artwork. Even after finishing my work, I occasionally return to that painting and add a few finishing touches. Sometimes, my painting feels so out of place that I completely alter it by painting over it.

Everyone has their own perspective of viewing an artwork – every artwork is an illusion. The painting is complete when you feel it is the closest you can get to the desired illusion. That is when you are satisfied with your work and declare it 'Finished.'

Final touches –

o Always view your painting in natural light, take a photo of it, and then look at the photo of your painting. Examining the painting from various angles will ensure that the color, density, and contrast are all as desired.

- o Make sure the base color extends to the side borders and corners. Occasionally, when using stretched canvas, I begin coloring the edges first.
- o If you don't paint the edges, the painting will appear incomplete from the side and it might also harm the canvas over time.

____

Varnish

Varnish is applied to the canvas to seal it. It shields the canvas from environmental irritants like UV rays, smoke, grime, and dust particles. This keeps the painting from fading or yellowing. It allows the artwork to last for many years and aids in the long-term preservation of the painting.

Varnish is available in two forms – Permanent and Removable. You can use a brush to apply varnish or purchase spray varnish.

Types –

  I.   Matte
  II.   Satin
  III.   Gloss

The Matte finish will lighten the deeper hue, Satin will soften it slightly, and Glossy varnish will highlight it. Less glare will be produced by matte and satin finishes than by gloss varnish. To achieve the desired shine level, you can also mix these varnish types.

If you wish to photograph your painting, do it before varnishing. When varnish is applied, it could reflect light and cause glare when capturing images.

Spray Varnish –

  o   Wipe down the painting's surface using a cloth.
  o   The room should be well-ventilated; alternatively, you can varnish your artwork in an outdoor space like a

garden, balcony, or terrace because varnish can release powerful fumes and odors.

- o The paint on the canvas needs to be entirely dried.
- o Put on a mask and cover your mouth and nostrils.
- o Lay out your artwork on a table flat.
- o Before putting varnish on the painting, shake the varnish bottle vigorously for a few seconds.
- o Apply the varnish in a vertical direction, covering the entire area.
- o After a minute, apply another layer in a horizontal direction to ensure complete coverage.
- o Two coats of spray paint are sufficient to protect the painting, but if you want a glossier finish, apply more layers.
- o Allow it to dry in a spotless, well-ventilated area so that the smell and fumes can quickly dissipate.

Isolation coat –

Applying an isolation coat will give a glass-like layer to the painting. It will function as a protective layer between your colors and Varnish. The isolation coat is permanent, and it may cause a slight variation in the color quality of the painting. Wait 4-6 hours before adding another coat if you are using many coats.

This coating is applied if you intend to later remove or replace the varnish. The centuries old art pieces are redeemed after replacing a layer of varnish.

Removable varnish coat –

- Wait 24 hours for the isolation coat to dry completely before varnishing.
- Acrylic paintings can be varnished with either oil or acrylic varnish. For oil paintings, only use oil varnish.
- The paint on the canvas must be entirely dry.
- To avoid inhaling fumes, wear a mask over your nose and mouth.
- The room should be well-ventilated; alternatively, you can varnish your artwork in an outdoor space like a garden, balcony, or terrace because varnish can release powerful fumes and odors.
- Dip a sizable, clean, and soft brush in varnish.
- Lay out your artwork on a table flat.
- Apply a thin layer vertically across the canvas, covering all sides and edges.
- After a short period of time, examine the painting from several angles to look for any spots that are less shiny or uneven.
- Apply additional coat if necessary to smooth out the surface.
- Allow it to dry in a spotless, well-ventilated area so that the smell and fumes can quickly vanish.
- Wash the brush with soap and water.

Epilogue

No one has all the answers. We never stop questioning what we know and what we need; we never stop exploring ourselves. Every question we answer leads to another.

The things which seem mundane, when seen from a different perspective, changes its meaning and reason for existence.

No one is right or wrong; everyone has a unique perspective. A painting on the wall may be meaningless for one person, while for another, it might signify everything.

When you paint, try to see things from your own perspective rather than from what you believe them to be. Every painting on a wall has a different meaning for each person.

Explore the infinite possibilities, rediscover your passion, and rediscover yourself without any constraints!

I'm an Artist at Living!
    ...And everyday I'm rediscovering who that is without a conditioned set of rules!

Jyoti Arora
Email: authorjyotiarora@gmail.com
Instagram: https://www.instagram.com/jyotiarorain

www.ingramcontent.com/pod-product-compliance
Lightning Source LLC
Chambersburg PA
CBHW040913110726
48005CB00006B/875